NOBODY'S PERFECT . . . BUT THIS IS RIDICULOUS!

Here comes the most lovable loser who ever got up on the wrong side of the bed. The creation of cartoonist Jim Unger, HERMAN is syndicated in more than three hundred newspapers throughout the world. Herman may have the blues, but he'll tickle you pink!

"FEELING RUN DOWN AGAIN, HERMAN?"

HERMAN

"FEELING RUN DOWN AGAIN, HERMAN?"

BY JIM UNGER

A SIGNET BOOK

NEW AMERICAN LIBRARY

PUBLISHED BY
THE NEW AMERICAN LIBRARY
OF CANADA LIMITED

Published by arrangement with Andrews, McMeel & Parker

The cartoons in *"FEELING RUN DOWN AGAIN, HERMAN?"*
all appeared originally in *The Second Herman Treasury*.

"Herman" is syndicated internationally by Universal Press
Syndicate.

First Printing, May 1986

2   3   4   5   6   7   8   9

SIGNET TRADEMARK REG. U.S. PAT. OFF. AND FOREIGN COUNTRIES
REGISTERED TRADEMARK—MARCA REGISTRADA
HECHO EN WINNIPEG, CANADA

SIGNET, SIGNET CLASSIC, MENTOR, PLUME, MERIDIAN
AND NAL BOOKS are published in Canada by The New American
Library of Canada, Limited, 81 Mack Avenue, Scarborough,
Ontario, Canada M1L 1M8

PRINTED IN CANADA
COVER PRINTED IN U.S.A.

"He can't get used to your new hairpiece."

"Take a look in here! Five bags of mail, two sets of encyclopedias and a brand-new vacuum cleaner."

"It's the airport! Your suitcase is in Alaska and
your brown bag is on the way to Singapore."

"Wake up, Dad."

"Gimme the keys to your company car!"

"The police towed away the car, so I
bought another one."

"Every time you press that buzzer,
just remember that I'm the one
who'll be taking out your stitches."

HIPPO

"Did you remember to send your mother a birthday card?"

"There's an elephant on TV and she's throwing
peanuts at it!"

"I claim this planet in the name of Bluggrovia."

"Sorry about your window, I'm practicing for
the Olympics."

"Excuse me for being born."

"If the house was on fire, who would you save
first, me or the cat?"

"I don't know what you're eating,
but you gave the dog a can
of spaghetti sauce!"

"What have you been feeding that parrot?"

"We can't elope. I haven't got a suitcase."

"Nothing your mother does surprises
me anymore."

"What's the big idea sticking this on the
back wall of the garage?"

"You're lucky you were wearing your seatbelt."

"Don't get any of that stuff on your father."

"Come down here. You've ruined my
plant."

"He's here now! Seal off the building."

"You do realize I'm going to have to report this, Thompson?"

"Boy! Did you see that ugly kid?"

"I gotta get new glasses! I thought
that was a big duck."

"I didn't see that. Did you get him with blueberry
or pecan?"

"I'm charging you a dollar for whatever it is you've got in your mouth."

"Dobson, I've just figured out a way for you personally to save this company $750 a month."

"You haven't signed these traveler's checks."

"Why didn't you say you wanted them both
the same size?"

"Look at your best shirt."

"It was in the freezer—must have thawed out!"

"You left that back door open again."

"Hey! Do you wanna see a U.F.O.?"

"Grandpa's bought an Afro wig."

"You can't rush my chunky stew."

"Phone the newspaper; I just found a second
piece of pork in this can of beans!"

"All the girls are off sick!"

"Don't blame the cat. What would you do if
someone sat on you?"

"If you want to see something 'real cheap,' take a look in the mirror."

"Put those back!"

"I just can't believe I'm gonna look like you when I'm 35."

"Grandma, you didn't borrow my sweater,
did you?"

"If this is gonna make me strong and handsome, I
think you'd better eat it."

"I'm going soon! Your house is always drafty."

"Folks, the main reason you're not getting a
good picture is because you bought yourselves
a microwave oven."

"Harry, quick, get over here."

"This is ridiculous! I raise you a nickel and you throw in four aces."

"Congratulations, Mrs. Parker."

"Don't forget to put his watch ahead
two hours. We forgot that last time."

"Throw them farther!"

"You left your wallet
at the fish shop!"

"I told you it wouldn't stay up there."

"No thank you. My husband's a
reformed wino!"

"I hate giving these injections. Look at my
hands shaking."

"What's the matter with you! Can't you save that for during the commercials?"

"Why are you such a messy eater?"

"Has that one got blue eyes?"

"Mr. Kelly, that man's here about the job. He looks
a bit drippy."

"How many times have I told you not to snap
your fingers while I'm extracting teeth
under hypnosis?"

"I guessed you weren't from around
here."

"I'm making her a coat the same as yours."

"Your sister's had another kid."

"Are you a good runner?"

"The basement's full of soapy water."

"He's glued his feet again."

"You've eaten all the nuts!"

"Would you say you are, 'extremely happy,'
'happy,' 'average' or 'bored stiff'?"

"Why would I marry you for your money? There must be easier ways for me to get my hands on 45 bucks!"

"Boy! I'm glad you're still awake. I was captured
by a UFO and taken to another planet."

"Nurse, run outside and
get his shoe."

"Why can't I have the movie on and you watch
the game during the commercials?"

"Is this the first time he's been outside today?"

"You're not gonna believe it·there's an
elephant coming."

"D'you get a lot of rain on your planet?"

"The kitchen's on fire again."

"Does he bite?"

"I found your birth certificate in the attic. You're not 54, you're 91."

"I've lost the use of my legs!"

"Don't forget, Buster. If it wasn't for me and Frankie
you'd be paying a lot more income tax."

"I told you not to jump around upstairs.
Look at my lamp!"

"Your aunt Frieda has left you $50,000 if you'll promise to look after her cat."

"Now snore."

"When you've got a minute, I'll have a box of parrot food."

"Don't make a face; it's cheaper than food."

"What was all that
screaming outside?"

"That must be one nervous parrot!"

"Just trim the sides and the back."

"Keep your eyes open.
Two prisoners are missing!"

"Are you wearing furry socks?"

"I don't know why I bother cooking for you!"

ABOUT THE AUTHOR

Jim Unger was born in London, England. After surviving the blitz bombings of World War II and two years in the British Army, followed by a short career as a London bobby and a driving instructor, he immigrated to Canada in 1968, where he became a newspaper graphic artist and editorial cartoonist. For three years running he won the Ontario Weekly Newspaper Association's "Cartoonist of the Year" award. In 1974 he began drawing HERMAN for the Universal Press Syndicate, with instant popularity. HERMAN is now enjoyed by 60 million daily and Sunday newspaper readers all around the world. His cartoon collections, THE HERMAN TREASURIES, became paperback bestsellers.

Jim Unger now lives in Nassau, Bahamas.